T0150666

the
moral
judgement
of
butterflies

k. eltinaé

PRAISE FOR THE MORAL JUDGEMENT OF BUTTERFLIES

This book's belief that "kindness exists despite / being quarantined on planes before arriving to your lands, / despite being interrogated," its belief in the possibility of healing "the cache of cities / built beneath our tongues" —is necessary. "I crawl into boxes / leave fingerprints // before I show you wings." Wings, indeed. This is a book of wings that we need and must give airspace to. Because they are inimitable and beautiful.

– ILYA KAMINSKY
author of *Deaf Republic* and *Dancing in Odessa*

This salient collection K.Eltinaé crafts a set of interconnected diasporic weavings that thread together the fragments of longing and belonging. There is a delicate lyricism and considered exploration throughout these poems that probe loss, not simply as a thing once had, but as a part of the human condition and the migratory reality of post-colonial Africans everywhere. Eltinaé's poems pull the reader into the inner-life of the poet and those who populate his world as a way for us to reimagine our own place in a relational revelation. This is a striking and necessary debut that reminds us we can make our world anew.

– MATTHEW SHENODA
author of *Tahrir Suite* and *The Way of The Earth*

This is the work of an artist who has touched the fire and emerged with survival scripts worthy of libation. This is poetry as life-saving instrument. This is poetry that matters.

– DIRIYE OSMAN
author of *Fairytales for Lost Children*

The Moral Judgement of Butterflies wends through cove and cave, tree shade and moonshine, aiming for the freedom of being at ease within the self, the total sovereignty found when one stops resisting "the vertigo of living." This is a startling collection of slow disappearances.

– LADAN OSMAN
author of *The Kitchen Dweller's Testimony* and *Exiles in Eden*

Between worlds feels like a no-man's-land, but sometimes it's the place where a poet is born.

– PHILIP METRES
author of *Shrapnel Maps & Sand Opera*

JUDGE'S CITATION

This poetry collection was nearly faultless in its imaginative reach, creative flair, and astonishing versatility. Reading it felt like being in the presence of an already-great vision, a writer (in this case) poet who knew precisely the measure of what had to be said, and why, but who never forgot that writing must be moving before it can be persuasive. I believe this collection will be one of the important books of this decade, and I am proud to have been able to select it.

– DR. TODD SWIFT, Judge of The International Beverly Prize for Literature

K. Eltinaé is a Sudanese poet of Nubian descent, raised internationally as a third culture kid. His work has been translated into Arabic, Greek, Farsi, and Spanish and has appeared in World Literature Today, The Ordinary Chaos of Being Human: Many Muslim Worlds (Penguin), The African American Review, About Place Journal, Muftah, among others. He is the first place poetry winner of Muftah's Creative Writing Competition *At Home in the World,* the winner of the Memorial Reza Abdoh Poetry Prize 2021 from Tofu Ink Press and the co-winner of the 2019 Dignity Not Detention Prize from Poetry International. He currently resides in Granada, Spain. More of his work can be found at:

🄵 https://www.facebook.com/eltinae/
🄾 https://www.instagram.com/k.eltinae

About the Illustrator: Abed El Moonem Omer a.k.a "Teddy Moonem" is a full-time artist from the ancient Omdurman region in Sudan. He studied economics and switched to art early in his career. He is a proud member of the Union of Fine Artists since 2008. His work has been exhibited in the German, British, and French cultural centers in Khartoum, and also in the city of Bahr Dar and Addis Ababa, Ethiopia.

First published in 2022
An Eyewear Publishing book, Black Spring Press Group
Grantully Road, Maida Vale, London W9, United Kingdom

Interior layout and graphic design by K. Eltinaé.
Typeset and symbols created by Hatim Eujayl.
Cover illustration by Carlos Martínez Aibar, Metamorphy.
Author photograph by Mario Pardo Segovia.
Interior illustrations by Abed El Moonem Omer.

ISBN: 978-1-913606-87-9

*The editor has generally followed American spelling
and punctuation at the author's request.*

BLACKSPRINGPRESSGROUP.COM

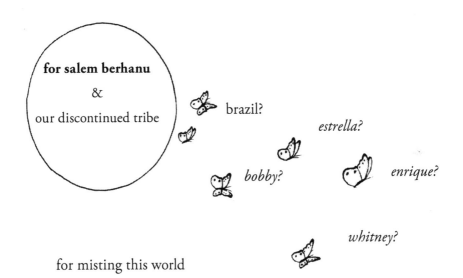

for salem berhanu

&

our discontinued tribe

brazil?

estrella?

bobby?

enrique?

whitney?

for misting this world

with your laughter.

p.s. ምንጣፍአለኝ

There is no place that cannot be home, nor is. — Audre Lorde

poems

 notes

In the same way sea turtles are born blindly in a place they can never belong to I have spent my life building nests between places my heart couldn't leave behind.

exile

Today
I will iron a shirt and face the wind.

Map out the city with my black taxi disguise,
listen to Indians, Africans and Arabs
claim my colors, hair and eyes.

Stopping for drinks, smiles, one-night stands
counting people holding hands gentler than mine.

Tomorrow
I will find a phone booth and call home,

listen to threats about the evils of wanderlust,
pretend I haven't survived them yet.

I will lie and tell them I am happy at last,
wait to hear that wherever I go,

walls have ears,
and from them I will never be free.

How much longer?

they still count days, months, years.
I think about those walls and their ears,

measuring every day how long it takes
to step out of the shower, tie laces, practice faces,

until I'm sent back to a place I fled
but never escaped.

here (how.everyone.remembers.everything)

k

this is the account of a broken boy who took down the   s   y

to weave a map for all the children on their way   *here.*

How do I have my Turkish mother's eyes that aren't blue like nazari beads, but the color of my father's skin when it has forgotten the sun because of winter? Family snapshot: the whole lot of us rubbing sesame oil into our skin to keep out the cold in all that gold we carried.

I'm broken, broken, and all you ask is how: *how did it happen? how can you be sure? how long will it take?* I count bubbles in your fizzy water make something up. I sigh and hear a thousand legs cross, I blink and imaginary hair parts me. Everyone 'getting by' is surviving something seasonal. It's out of stock before you break each other for some mess that won't ever hold you both.

I'm so sorry about so many things I can't ever be again. It doesn't stop me from looking under the bed some nights for change. Doesn't stop me from polishing the mirror until I sigh again and armies march through the flat like it's over.

Your tongue is now that kilim draped from the balcony for wandering cats. It still remembers when it lived inside and how we whispered Hafez verses to it. Everything I bought for that next life is on sale, but I still don't fit.

native

All those rights I was taught about
never apply in airports.

I'm ushered into a room
where everything I could fit from home

is handled by men who touch the same kind of things
but forget where cotton and gold came from.

I crawl into boxes
leave fingerprints

before I show you wings
nobody taught you about.

settle

I wonder what they told themselves
when dust settled under carpets in lands
where clove, mint and cinnamon
turned to soot like smell and taste.

Why was I too young to remember anything
but how my parents argued in the car
over the phone bill?

So thirty years later
when I get harangued about distance,
about forgetting where I come from,

I remind myself that
a few dial tones away from every *how*, *when* and *why* is a dagger.

How far I felt those fingers
searching for illegalities
I carried always in my heart.

How I sat through fourteen lectures in a language
I could barely follow, and felt more at home than ever.

How after dinner for the first month abroad
I stitched the fluffy gut back into that floral duvet,
how the customs officer gently unwrapped it on a steel table
before cutting it open, waiting for something there to glow.

Why then do our answers about love only survive in pictures?
Why can a voice hijack so many passengers but never quietly land?

ltd. (letters.that.drag)

For ح, who danced himself out of the war with jackal laughter,
in love with a different woman every night
to wake up alive in the morning.

For ز, who filled her basement with my books in Omdurman
when I went back and found no home to rest in.

For و, who made the earth move with smiles,
waiting till takeoff to toast with me on a plane out of Khartoum
full of men and women who judged and cursed our freedom.

For ف, whose half-closed eyes ruined every school photo,
loving everything at five percent in case it disappeared.

For أ, and for the girl he loved whose parents wouldn't
claim her body at the morgue and bury her
because they were found together.

For ل, whose cave embraces from the blue city,
for almonds and dates and shade from every passing word
for every act of love that travels timeless as a seed.

For ح, who died at twenty-six, missile launched by the regime
into his bedroom, for his family whose grief was muted
when they named him a martyr.

For ر, whose laughter still rings in my ears
though she died at a teaching hospital.
Whose day came when glucose and saline
were confused by a doctor
living in a country where death is never questioned.

Each of these letters
drag me back to a place
I can't believe I survived.

breathing exercise

It's a full moon, so I rise to the occasion; end up at a bar called *Estrella,* if that makes any sense. You're there pouting in your black dress. It's been a few months and you say I *abandoned* you. *Abandoned* is what fanatics did to the faith I was raised in, when they tore up the sky and left a city of rubble from a word like surrender. But you're ok. You're doing yoga now; your body is a temple. I think about how many I've buried in mine. Abandoned is *how* I left home. Left my sister and younger brother to pack up their lives as they caved, when the last home we knew disappeared under a word like greed. Everything else that came after the country I fled to, rusted like an anchor and quit being a choice.

I'm a goddess you say, *I need a god* and all I can think of are my parents, those *inshallah* futures I cannot share with them because we are not the same people. I can't remember the word in Turkish for forget, only "remember": *hatırlamak.*

Hatırlamak lifting your aunt
from her bed into her wheelchair after she lost both legs.
How proud you were of those first veins that popped up
before your body was mapped with them.
Hatırlamak how your parents joked about you dying of patience
until you did, though no one mourned.
Hatırlamak how your whole body went ripe that time you heard
someone say *Go home,* 'cause you knew you needed a new address every
time you landed.

Forgetting in Arabic is human, a collective act of omission that sinks

e

n

s

a

In Greek, lismonó (λησμονώ) *forget* is a pigeonhole we crawl into
to escape the vertigo of living.

Ensa that accent that rises like a pyramid in your throat
every time they mention home.

Lismonó those who claim studying and living somewhere
are not the same thing.

Hatırlamak you belong anywhere you can flee to
and return from in one piece.

Hatırlamak your language will follow you
even into the bed of a stranger with no tongue.

Ensa the way some scents invade and bomb your insides
like a gas that puts you under.

Lismonó your nest sometimes...

Hatırlamak we are born borderless until we touch.

kohl

Is it still called asylum
when you race amid nightfall
setting camp under your own dust,
half dreaming you're a zebra
because the marrow in your bones
won't settle for a land?

And what about the fear
strangers paint across faces

whenever you cough or share a path?

Who will defend the maps
taken from the truth by lies?

Who will trace the kohl for our eyes?

bloom

It began with trees

etched with so many things
that lived and fought to fill a space

in that tomb
we call heart.

I cry white and blue,
question if I'm here to father

more lives, before I am ready
to age in one place.

The wind scatters my tears,
laughs like a *djinn* in the fields
when they bloom.

watermark

Something happens
when you lose all your family to a word.

When you finally choose sky over light, cloud
over howling and slow disappearance.

She calls herself sister
though she is more like a radicalized cousin
who disappeared on a bus
and only hears herself now.

A colorblind brother lurks
says he won't fire
unless he smells blood, life or sorrow.
So where do I hide them?

First try your father
who raised you Arab and *free*
free of what? you ask him

Comb your hair, always
leave the house with your afro
people will remember that.

A mother's confession singes:

I should've let you go... waited for that heartbeat
to drown instead of birthing you
only to hang like a teardrop from both of my eyes.

One of my teeth won't bleach

Look! he says *there's a brown streak*
and a blue one...I've never seen anything like it.

I think of both Niles
of the person I drowned there.

daughterland

On August 15th 2018, twenty-four school children drowned on their way to school near Meroe, Sudan when their boat capsized in a strong current during flooding season. Most of the children onboard were girls. Some families lost all their children.

Because every seed was planted م by a god or man
who thought himself one,
all we have ever passed down
to survive
is war.

What happened to that dagger
you buried outside in case they showed up
to steal your mother-tongue?
That خ in your first name
that slit throats until danger passed.

        ي was a boat

carrying school children
who were only taught
to swim on land.

Twenty-four
one for every hour and sky I look out at

                                                  ر

They are half moons   everywhere
even under my eyes in the morning.
My hands cup water that travels down wrong,
people   stare on as I choke.

ام can be mother or a spinning head.
Sometimes you have to choose between
weeping in the lap of a stranger
or a compass.

Ninety thousand men, women and children
dragged their dust to rivers dams were never built for.
Under six cataracts lie the bones of my ancestors
slaves, because the sun charred their skin
and made raisins of their hearts.

heimat 𝇋

(a) a place ▮
(b) I was ▮ in ▮
(c) there are many places in this place
(d) when I was a child ▮
(e) I felt ▮
(f) ▮ nothing ▮ could happen to me
(g) I can't feel like this in any other places
(h) because ▮
▮ .
(j) these places are not like any other ▮
(k) I was ▮ a part of.
(l) I can't be ▮ a part of any other ▮
(m) this place is ▮ part of me
(n) ▮ other people think the same ▮ about these places)
(o) ▮
(p) (when I think about these people, I feel something) ▮

tirhal

There was a time
before borders and stamps decided where we came from.

We welcomed births and grievances over teas,
measured departures with stories,
dust that followed us everywhere.

Voices rose and scattered people like an earthquake,
before prayer in the hearts of men and women disappeared
like bread and water.

On the morning a traveler set out,
he left two footprints behind.

One that faced the path he was taking,
another that gave him one last glimpse of home
before it changed forever.

There are boundless events,
which precede that first cry
before a new life bursts forth and the cord is slashed.

Before first steps and comparisons
to dead and living relatives are made,
our futures shift recalibrating destiny.

We were born to chase our truths in transit.

ceremony

Ten goddesses
dance across lines and mounts

chest against chest in that hollow place
where air is worshipped.

Joined by birds in the throats of women
who honor tragedies and disappearing landmarks.

Joyful arms plead with the sky for evenings of breeze
where shuffling feet, snapping fingers

and the clamor of bangles
beg like prophets, to be heard.

atlas

My mother taught me
how to drag rumors through the desert

make them disappear like men
who pretend to have no teeth.

She showed me how to split barbwire,
bury its pain in coves I never could find again.

Some mornings I find myself
tilting like those jars of honey she bought

waiting for that bubble to surface
and swallow my doubts before moving on.

kismet

He could have been my father,
with his blue-black skin

asking directions in that language
that wiped us off the map.

He could have been my father
with his safari suit and silver rings

with vowels clipped and buried
so no one would hear them sing.

I cough up sand and answer:

I am the son of a dove and a panther
from their blood and feathers
I have learned about love.

He could have been my father,
but he smiled when he talked about God.

dowry

They do no milieu justice
the rapturous things we learn to be true

hanging like jasmine
on a summer night.

Resentful walls claim weight
of legacies we assume, not because
time unearthed them, but from the shame we fear
the gossip of borders.

We wait too long for dowries,
for the sweat of strangers
to remember our own perfume.

talisman

When glass shattered
something evil had passed

by and not through us.
So we swept up the mess

believed ourselves lucky until
what followed for years.

still-born

Was she dancing or counting bodies in her language?

Go on, tell her about how you still can't
look at a belt without remembering the weight
and moaning across the carpet.

How your clothes still kiss the floor
and age faster than you sleep.

Choose all you want she says,
but live under my feet.

forgiveness

I bear arms to protect myself from in-between things
like flying or drowning or bursting in flames.

Crawling into the belly of a whale
spat out in some seaport where my tongue
won't curl the same.

I bear memories of doors
that brought visitors in the evenings,
feet that twitched as secrets spilled.

Waiting years to forget
the heat of last words,
the senseless tears we shed.

snake

One day your hope
will grow fingers;

a spirit you can wrestle
as soon as windows are discovered.

Heart fluttering over months
as he shoots past your thighs
then waist and shoulders

into a breathing moving mountain
you admire at breakfast.

You wait for those years
when he will worry about things

like clothes and pleasing people on the outside
before you tell him about being a snake.

What if you wait too long,
years after he learns at school about hunger
about Africa from posters,
about the darkness of wilderness and crime?

What if he talks back and you want to answer
that he sounds like every man
who damned and cursed you,

every man you forgave
to make that life for him?

unconditional

I choose the seat closest to the door
in case someone steps off
I can follow out and start a new life with.

Instead, I meet couples who are travelling
who speak about 'home' and getting 'back' to places
I cross off the map.

What if I told her my first kiss was on a staircase
at school between classes, that I lost my balance
and that each time love has felt that way?

What if I told them I still walk around
with imaginary *djinns* on my shoulders
that weigh like shame from childhood

that I bow my head to and offer things
I have never had without asking?

What if I dream of being met by a stranger
who sees me in the way I cannot?

I want her to forgive me for leaving.
For slipping home into a safe I've forgotten how to use.

&

for Samah Alhadi

On March 23rd 2021, Samah Alhadi's life was brutally taken by her father in the city of Omdurman, Sudan after attempting to flee her home. Her body was buried following her family's wishes to not have an autopsy performed. The official cause of death was that she had been killed by a stray bullet and was later changed to suicide. The diener confirmed that Samah had been beaten all over her body. The remaining members of her immediate family stood silent until days later an investigation was launched by Human Rights Activist Dr. Nahid Jabralla.

A chorus of daughters
born once
to valueless men
        gather
          to play the song of &.

      did anyone
   hear their light before
          lives were towed
     into memories that
         pool in the throat.
                  شيل شبابي
        They sing
      شيل عينيا

   I am watching our children
crawling through clouds
        to the feet of a chorus singing ارحم شوية

        و اهدي لي لحظات near a lake
where every kora playing شيل باقي عمري
        شيل شبابي
         is an &
             we can't afford.

nefsi

You mustn't beg for love.
Wave it down for the rush it gives
or the places you discover together.

Don't look for neighbors in your silence
for that noise that distracts
from the breathing of your own life,
though it's sleepless as a nightingale.

You shouldn't yearn
for eight arms and longer breath underwater
for small silver smiles that expire tomorrow.

Never bow your head to loveless duties
those mirages you were taught to chase alone
while others walked their path.

You mustn't pine for a love
you can nurse like a wound, trace back the life
in its scars, confide in, and still look after in your mind.

You mustn't mine for love, petrol or diamonds.
Tend to the wealth and splendor in your laughter.
Be selfish with your love.

Stock, simmer, seal it in jars
for winter, all year long.

Keep your love.

Be thankful of its scent on walls and sheets, in pantries.
Lather in your love at home
before you decide someone else is more deserving.

Whisper *Nefsi*
as you hang laundry
feel that love spread from your shoulders.

bolanile

You step out of the shower
supple like grapes and coconuts.

I cannot shave in the fog
you've made, so I listen

to the kettle in the kitchen
waiting for a face to emerge.

I rinse out sugar and mint
taste home on your lips
before it disappears.

tusk

for S.S

He caught her smiling
said her teeth were ivory,

so she hid how
every kind of love

came and went like
the power-lines.

Sometimes
she stands behind mothers at the supermarket

dreaming of joining them,
belly-carved with poems unfolding.

Sometimes
there is a man holding her at night
worrying about the future, and some nights

her poems hold her up against the sky
under eyelids like a tusk.

ostrich

I still dream about my brothers,
their laughter and cologne at night.

Before eyelashes and youth vanished
like melon seeds parted joyfully on lips.

Before lives were arched like pillows
bent and handled by so many stories

we stopped listening to the voice
and compass of our fingers.

My heart is weighed against an ostrich feather
after weeks of grapefruits and incense

I am ready to leave again.

Imagined and longed for conversations
weigh more than anyone I've left behind.

fulani blues

I have a hard time telling mother
she should get out and exercise
so we talk about people she admires for hours.

Fulan al fulani's son married a girl
he saw on his uncle's wedding dvd.
Took them three weeks to ask about the family,
will you come for the wedding?

Fulan al fulani's son has a son now,
named after his late father
too much sugar in our blood, the heat, mosquitos
take the best ones early
what keeps you there... when here is better?

She calls after work excited
has met a girl with dimples
ready to *start a family with a modest man*
willing to marry a stranger
who barely lives with himself.

gauze

I am almost ready to forget
the noose your father made

the day he warned you
to stop being yourself.

The funeral of everything
buried that year you quit

watching television
so you could always remember.

We are both
free of every floating version of ourselves,

we can now roll as gauze
to heal the cache of cities
built beneath our tongues.

forget

I allude to birthmarks and scars
when you ask where I'm from

because speaking about it
makes life now sound make-believe.

You go back to yours, nap after lunch.
I do laundry and listen to Om Kalsoum

to that verse about smoldering wine
from her lover's hand and dream.

You drop by my apartment
laugh about the incense and smoke

we wander the city,
pass by new places

stopping with the same people
grateful to hear our names remembered somewhere.

suitor

for I.A.

You sent her back
because she ate like fire and bore no children.

Because the world you were raised in
taught you broken things were best returned.

Do you think about how she is still moving through life
like a paperweight, medicated for the hunger of longing,

thirsty for a 'love that came after'
you could never provide?

She seldom talks about it.
Just carries on loving

in her broken way
unfinished things

it's sad how after three divorces,
people think *you* are the problem

not the society
that asks a girl to find love
where it won't exist.

balcony

I want to hold the truth between us
but there's no currency for love in memories like ours.

Describe the home where you grew up
I'm asked on the form and all I remember are stairs.

Bodies slumped like burlap sacks shifting under my feet
counting in English, Arabic, Greek

until I am back pacing on that balcony holding my father's hand
as he shows me the world for the first and last time.

Forget the view, stay close he says,
so I built ladders in our silence,
tunnels until it was behind me.

Love swallows to protect mother says
as one by one we went missing.

I want to hold the truth between us
to survive love without running.

then

All that I know about kneeling
comes from the ground where I was left
to dig until new maps came.

Memory sits barefoot on a doorstep
sewing patches as the moon yawns.

When I want you, your voice goes missing
like blood in disappearing veins.

Where is that musk of doorways,
those clouds we clung to as we chartered the sky?

What else is loneliness but a lover smoking on a ledge
near a bed that always smells of *then*?

I find a terrace seat at a neighboring cafe, and begin drawing a line of pyramids in gold first, then purple, and black, before a friendly waiter takes my order. When he returns he asks if I'm drawing a fence or a border; I decide it's best not to tell him I'm drawing home. The classical Arabic word for 'home': دار is the same as the Spanish verb for 'give': dar. So what exactly has home given me?

διαφορετικός

When I fainted at the fish market
doctors blamed the smell.

When it happened again,
samaritan aunts and uncles came to visit

whispering kind things,
as they waited for me to die.

When I didn't, they called me names
they couldn't take back
until their children were born different.

sanctuary

And I have known for some time now
that happiness would come
once one of us has gone.

And though we are born
dreaming of storks who deliver us
sometimes lineage engulfs a face while it sleeps.

Maybe in-betweenness
puts you two steps behind
when you learn to be selfish about company

when so many of us expire with longing
swollen on shores like motherless whales.

We seek peace in one place
until we learn that sanctuaries exist
without birds that ascend
in a way we cannot follow.

the خ in my life

I am fine with forgetting that خ sound
tearing joyfully like pants or a body surrendering to sleep.

How many words are missing in my life
like goodness (خير) and destruction (خراب)
cucumbers (خيار) and choice (اختيار).
I am finally free of fear (خوف) and differences (اختلافات)
manners (أخلاق) and bread (خبز).
I lose words like brother (أخ) and sister (أخت),
can no longer say I've had enough (خلاص)
in my own head without mixing identity with language.

In Khartoum (الخرطوم) they call me Arab.
Arab there *equals* light-skinned *meaning* free of slave ancestry.

In Arabia, I am too Black to be related to the prophet
but my name and language grant me a community
that calls me slave behind my back.

The Arabic word for shit
like my name begins with (خ)
which is why you can keep them both.

zemiru HgᵒႱ

Distance yourself from evil and sing to it. – Arabic proverb

The problem with language
begins with love we bury in children forever.

First I put a compass
between your lips and my footsteps

so everyone you lied to
could see which one of us got lost.

All the gardens I remember
exist now in worn-out stories

so rooted is their sadness
I dent sofas when I recall

how hard I threw your envy into the ocean.
How long I waited for the waves that stopped,

how far my heart floated
pale and dizzy carried away by birds.

Your face
that broken plate I keep
to remember how to sing.

hüzün

In memory of Mahasin Agha

It isn't GRIEF, came out too loudly
made a few of them uncomfortable,
crossing arms and feet under chairs.

How do I tell them that so many words
in their language rattle like cages without birds?

That 'understanding' for you is a perception,
and for us it springs from 'knowledge.'

Do I tell them about Mahasin?
Who rushed to witness my birth
in a sparkling green tobe that drew too much attention at the airport.

How she was scolded for it on the way to the hospital
by my uncle, the baby brother she raised,
who when she died, only sent money for arrangements.

Do I tell them how memories come
in purple, red, green and gold,

the colors she wore when she lit incense
and laughter throughout the house
dancing when men were not around?

Do I confess we failed at consoling mother
who gave away nail polish after the funeral,

cut the long thick hair she used to sit on
that never grew back?

Do you call it grief
when the nest you fall from disappears into the sky

and your lungs collapse with
the sillage of a memory that will never be done?

That isn't grief for us,
we call that hüzün.

65

enough

Let us not speak of waterfalls tonight
of bodies lost in rivers, unaccounted for.

Only having said that, is already too much.

Enough to turn off the television,
and call a friend to meet for a drink.

Enough to count yourself blessed
to have someone who sees you as 'enough'
because you mirror that and call it love.

Well then tell me, how can we help those people?

My pride begs to answer *Go, help yourself first,*
but isn't that how we ended up, divided by

light/rich/here | | **dark/poor/there,**
myths about skin and privilege?

All my dreams are about people being freed
from the violence of water slapping rock

from the burden of living on a land
knowing different, but not believing out-loud.

madame

I will always remember you in a nightgown
moving in and out of marriages like an ebony ghost.

My family lay out pictures from different years
to explain evolution and destruction all at once.

I am suddenly at the funeral of your first husband
who died in his early twenties of an overdose

left you with a fortune you put to good use
traveling the length of Europe with that mouth

a nest of pearls that made men drunk.
The second disappeared, so you started writing blank checks

out of grief in his name until they caught you at the airport.
So when you married the lawyer who later left you everything,

you were ready to love the Arab banker
who consoled you at his funeral

who bought the matching suitcases you left at a friend's
before his car went over a cliff almost a year later.

You signed for everything
and later moved back to Khartoum

into a house bigger than that loneliness;
spent your last days a welcome guest at funerals

a smiling moon
that spun men into dust.

as long as you want

As long as there are pilgrimages
from heart to tongue and back
there will always be hours for mercy.

If you can pick up thirty years later,
kiss and meet the skin you left
feel that part of you returning,
there will still be years for new laughter.

As long as you want without understanding,
you will forever chase naked and barefoot children
who will not follow out of fear or rain.

pride

My baby will not speak.
Twice a week outside a room

I watch him draw a past
I've buried in hues of purple, blue, and green.

Deep-set eyes and hollow cheeks
the doctors make no sense of.

Nests of broken hair
and nails float in the water

and will not forgive me,
but he listens and understands why.

My baby won't test his feet
breaking hearts and plastic wheels that push too hard.

I dread the morning he'll find his wings
and drift the way I had to.

mute

The oldest woman in our village
had fingers missing on her left hand.

All because she waved her hands at the sky
on the day she lost her son
wailed that no God was left for her.

If her voice before was
veiled like a recurring night,

she was done whispering at a family
who gave her away like perishing fruit.

Today women are birthing turtles
from the honey in their wombs into this world.

Crawling away from the center
our future loses force as do traditions.

tideline

Moving with all this silence
I forget the weight of the tideline
as I follow God into the water.

I'm repeating prayers from religion class,
the ones people swore

destroyed fear and brought on miracles and triumph.
I struggle against two arms speaking in one voice,

dragging me back
to honor the drum of living.

arraigo

My aunt is still alive
scheduling Eid lunches out-loud to soothe away panic
I am transfixed by the mallow leaves in her hands
how like worry they multiply then disappear.

The social worker is taking notes across the room.

Mother is propped on a cushion at the far end of my breath
legs crossed counting currency
έντεκα, είκοσι ένα, τριάντα ένα.

Only the last three years will be considered
she tells me after living here for ten
I need more proof   *you*
                    belong
              here.

Open my mouth
as a ghost talks about the weight of my life,
each year, invisible, undocumented.
she nods, says
        I need receipts   فاتورة
                              we say back home
I want to grab the alif أ
tap the earth between us and deliver them,
like a miracle but the word now spells فتُور
at my feet a dizzy ة pirouettes, a coin
I toss back to mother who claims it was stolen.

kendine dikkat et oğlum she snaps when I talk back
ببيعك وبشتريك   father says without thinking, if challenged.

Where do your parents live now?
Father is watching National Geographic sipping hibiscus
each bunion is a compass begging me
to flee the room.

Her phone rings and I hear mother's classic *Τι διάολο θέλεις τώρα;*
leave the office promising to hand over proof
I've existed for years.

Have you ever cried about something so vast, you could not begin to describe it? A looming threat so enveloping, that all you feel is a kind of suffocation, a premonition that at any minute you could be swallowed, forgotten and made invisible by force.

when you find your self
    they   body

what they **call** you is / dirty / dangerous / deadly / disposable / deranged

did you come from the jungle / they ask about **your** lips

if people read your books down there.   hair

Did your parents fall in love first or were they paired to breed/
            more mouths to feed/ brown bodies surrendering/ soil thick with
                  us/
                  them,
                    us/them,
                  us/
                  stacks/
            were we created to serve/to know our place is nowhere?

what you **call** yourself in that language brother?/ are you other?/

You are not just a dead blank stare.

Don't ever hate **your** skin   Please *know* you come from everywhere.

                  hair.
Please forget that body. you're on the road now, no one is waiting. what's left of you is a bus.

            wheel is a person you wouldn't leave behind.
every one onboard is blindfolded and crying for their mother
      mother is a bus stop you swerve past to get home.

you **call** those mothers/trees.

        the passengers crying/wind.
            When police ask if your ID is valid they mean *you deserve to die.*
They start shooting all the passengers you carry. The police aren't safe until they torch it.
They step back and watch everything you love, shrinking covered in glass and blood.
            We always migrate to a place where everyone
                  is alive inside/resisting.

tomorrow

I watch them returning to Allah
headlines of hope and despair

and I burn toast, burn rice, burn my hands
I cannot look away *because* I am away.

Some nights I press unlock
in some dreamed-up parking lot

and different cars are waiting to take me
but I've buried street names and exits,
all the shortcuts I knew
in a wallet I quit using ten years ago.

I have forgotten the weight
of carrying four names

all this time here, lost,
I've been surviving with two.

waif

I didn't tell you about it because somewhere some faraway
distant third cousin removed is on the other end of the receiver

      sinking

            the fantasy of

                                   h

                               o

                                 m

                              e

with so many secrets I can never open up about.

Because that iceberg in my throat makes me
and everything I love sound homesick and foolish

when all I want to feel is my own sweat drying
on those temporary countries that map a body
while it is running away.

      All I want is to sit on benches, stretch my bridges
celebrate freedom in a house near a river with no telephones.

bounty

I don't remember what it felt like before
that shot in the arm ate my soul up.

Your children count sheep
that disappear into the sky,

I count the lives lost to Ebola
someone believed deserved to die.

plans

Every time I say *yes* – I return,
feel fingers in a battlefield
divvying land on my arms and chest.

You want to build something with my lips
over memories when we sleep
so I tell the truth.

Sometimes I think
my hope is living elsewhere.
A single mom raising children
who communicate in sign language.

I know
my passport is a sign people miss on the highway
& swear was never there until they count every visa
I've overstayed & start pointing fingers.

I believe
we all come back
from this life as the cats in Istanbul.

I need
you to understand that all we will ever be are immigrants
that when the land recedes, the water won't know
the color of our skin, but our bones will.

Sometimes I want
to visit and settle in love but there are land-mines
at the border leading to every fantasy.

Sometimes if you look
hard enough at something it will bloom in your eyes &
make countries for refugees no one took in.

freedom

This poem is open as in open fire
as in one hundred and eighteen lives lost

peacefully protesting on June 3rd 2019
and the world hardly blinked.

How do I say *sorry* in your language?
Sorry not like *for your loss* but that
we walk the same earth, even breathe the same air
sorry that our bodies are dragged to rivers today
and remain uncounted tomorrow?

My heart goes...out
to the cafe or a bar or some mall downtown...

How far outside yourself
have you ever really gone for a stranger?

How do I say *internet blackout*
in a way that makes you visualize
people disappearing, now, like during your lunch break
lives changing from is to *was*
faster than you do before you hit the gym.

Where does your peace live, brother?
Can mine visit soon?

Can't we all want the same things
even if we look different?

paradise

I found no paradise
in the faces of the beggars

who accepted alms and prayed for you
at the mosque until I disappeared.

Spent weeks in that apartment, windows sealed off
sleeping with your scent until I couldn't.

Woke up in a fisherman's net
born again not from love but duty.

I break salt on the rocks by the gates
hear your laughter in that garden
oblivious of bars.

illegal

I am waiting for a paper to be free,
a stamp left and right on my chest
to bring back a hundred miracles.

I dream about hands at night curved around a pen,
dream about what currencies I've been.

Tattered suitcase at some airport,
frail but standing on a conveyer belt;
that's exactly how I felt when you called me *illegal*.

All these white God appointments
are auditions for the other side

our people still hunted for teeth and skin.
Is everybody/nowhere welcoming?

They say for every child aborted
a refugee crosses the Mediterranean.

Kiss my pillow for safe passage through the night,
kiss the trees that fall so I can dream of standing.

wasiya وصية

How long is a life avoiding the beach? believing God spoke through my father/some found seashell pushed off a shelf I cannot bury/I'd like to think there are aisles of men praying somewhere once I'm gone/that their tongues wrap around where I kept warm like a turban woven in prayer by strangers/that I am not found stiff/half hanging off a hotel bed under a phrasebook in another useless language/I hope I go dreaming in Arabic/because love there sounds like the wind passes through every vowel/somewhere buried in my voice there is asphalt singing as brothers build rooms for one another/I find new corners in case I come back/everyone gets a *duaa* to float across the lake and watch disappear/this is mine.

kindness

We are still dreaming of a vacation
from being chased out of cities.

For the empathy every child dangles
in their mother's eyes as hope.

For a future where the 'other' challenges every fear
we unlearn and accept to grow from.

One day you too will face that same floor
you pressed a man's face against before you handcuffed him.

You too will cry futile tears to keep living.
The difference is your dignity

will never know cages
and days without showering

will never know the shame
of running from a place

you are forced to return to
because you weren't born disposable.

If you feel threatened about living in a country
full of sleek, dark and beautiful bodies

arriving on boats smiling and glowing
though nobody has welcomed them,

stop watching the news.

This poem is for you,
for your parents
and their parents too.

For children
who should learn from the different
looking, speaking, believing 'other'

whose kindness exists despite
being quarantined on planes before arriving to your lands,

despite being interrogated and segregated in queues at the airport
for your precious safety.

Stay safe, with truths that bloom from kindness.

butterflies

I am sitting in a bar somewhere with a few friends and people I've just met. Their eyes are glittering with laughter after I tell them about growing up with a dad with a public and private English accent. About how at work in his crisp white doctor's coat he spoke in a kind and friendly, all-American way. How everyone loves him for his easygoing conversations and humor, his agility with learning languages like Urdu and Tagalog from staff that disappeared as soon as he got home.

At home, Sudan TV is blaring in the background with people dancing around whatever really needs to be said because people are way too polite to each other for no damn reason. I do not mention to anyone afterwards that I have been living in exile since I was eight. I order a new drink and decide to sit back and listen in case his voice returns to chase me home.

For mother's day, our teacher asked us to write poems to read on stage for them after they had dinner. It took the effort of four other classmates and me to push the velvet curtain far enough to one side to get a peeking view of all the tables set up in our middle school gym. Piled against each other we took turns pointing out our moms. When I found mine, dressed in a colorful traditional tobe they all asked me if I was adopted and I started to cry and refused to read my poem. She came backstage and shook me by the shoulders straightening my shirt and warned me in a few languages my teacher couldn't understand not to embarrass myself, that everyone would be watching. So I got on stage and read my poem to someone make-believe in the crowd.

It's summer and I'm at a friend's house drinking horchata. This creamy tiger nut milk concoction that makes me rambly and nostalgic. My friend's mom asks to see photos of my family and I show her pictures of my parents in the early seventies before they met each other, before any of us existed. She marvels at how stunning they were in their youth. Then I show her pictures of my siblings.

Only I know that every photo is at least a decade old. That we are all now very different people, but I was the first to leave.

You must miss them, she says. I say of course out loud in Spanish, ¡Por supuesto! Hear them arguing all at once in my mind as I tuck them back into a folded pocket in my wallet, repeating to myself لعب, φυσικά, tabii ki, bien sûr, certo. Of course we miss what we choose to remember.

At the airport I am interrogated by three men. One asks in broken English how long I've been here, the other scans my passport and stares me down. The third is having lunch and typing some kind of report. I am imagining the measurements being taken in a separate room, with all this information. Wait for a sheet of double-glazed shatterproof glass, 178 cm fitted stainless steel frame to arrive through the door. Wait for him to stop talking, for that pin to trap me forever in one place. I have waited my entire life to come out of this.

My entire life to fly away.

Acknowledgment and gratitude is due to the editors of the following print and online publications where many of these poems appeared in earlier versions:

World Literature Today, Poetry International, The International Poetry Review, The African American Review, About Place Journal, Muftah, Michigan Quarterly Review, Tofu Ink Press, The Other Side of Hope, Poetry Potion, Sawti Project, Foreign Literary, Pyriscence, Xavier Review, Muftah, Sons & Daughters, Burning House Press, The Ordinary Chaos of Being Human: Tales from Many Muslim Worlds, Jaffat El Aqlam, Sukoon, Solidago, Rigorous, New Contrast, Poetry Potion, Word Fountain, Baphash Literary & Arts Quarterly, Scintilla, TRACK// FOUR, Paperbark, Persian Sugar in English Tea Volume III, Surrealist/ Outsider Anthology by Thrice Press, The WAiF Project, Illya's Honey, Elsewhere Literary Journal, The Ofi Press, NILVX, Ink in Thirds, Zin Daily, The Elephants, Algebra of Owls, Poetic Diversity, Chanterelle's Notebook, and *Poetry Pages.*

& is a logogram and symbol also used as an indication of the future.

شيل شبابي in Arabic translates to *take my youth*.

شيل عينيا in Arabic translates to *take my eyes*.

ارحم شوية in Arabic translates to *show us some mercy*.

و اهدي لي لحظات in Arabic translates to *bestow me with moments*.

شيل باقي عمري in Arabic translates to *take what remains of my life*.

arraigo is the Spanish word for *rooted*.

έντεκα, είκοσι ένα, τριάντα ένα in Greek translates to *11, 21, 31*.

فاتورة is an Arabic word for *receipts*.

فُتور in Arabic translates to *apathy, exhaustion*.

kendine dikkat et oğlum is the Turkish expression for *watch yourself, boy*.

ببيعك وبشتريك in Arabic translates to *I will sell and buy you if I please*.

Τι διάολο θέλεις τώρα in Greek translates to *What the hell do you want now?*

breathing exercise

ensa is an Arabic word for *forget*.

hatırlamak is the Turkish word for *remember*.

inshallah is an Arabic expression which translates to *God willing*.

lismonó (λησμονώ) is a Greek word, meaning both *forget* and *pigeonhole*.

bolanile is a (Yoruba) Nigerian name meaning *the wealth of a home*.

djinns are intelligent spirits of lower rank than the angels, able to appear in human and animal forms to possess humans.

duaa is the Arabic word for *prayer*.

διαφορετικός is the Greek word for *different*.

fulani is a primarily Muslim people scattered throughout many parts of West Africa to the Atlantic coast. It is also an expression used widely in the Arabic speaking world to refer to an absent someone usually used as *fulan al fulani*.

heimat is a German word with no English equivalent that denotes the relationship of a human being towards a certain spatial social unit. The term forms a contrast to social alienation and usually carries positive connotations. It is often expressed with terms such as *home* or *homeland*.

hüzün is an Arabic word also used in Turkish to describe a hue of sadness or melancholy resulting from inadequacy or failure and weighing so heavily that it becomes communal, resigned, and even curiously poetic.

kismet comes from the Arabic word, meaning *division, portion, lot*. An event that will inevitably happen, destined for you as part of your fate.

kohl is a black powder widely used in the Middle East and North Africa to contour or darken the eyelids and as protection from the evil eye.

nefsi is an Arabic word which has a double meaning: nefsi means *my soul* and *my own self*.

tirhal is an Arabic word for *decampment*, the act of leaving your place for another, the state of moving, travelling in the Bedouin, nomadic sense from place to place.

tobe is an outer garment worn in some parts of North and Central Africa, consisting of a length of cloth draped over one shoulder and wrapped around the body.

wasiya is the Arabic word for *last will* or *testament*.

zemiru(ዘምሩ) is an Amharic word for *sing* in the imperative form.

The epigraph is taken from the poem "School Note." by Audre Lorde, *The Black Unicorn*: Poems, 55. New York: Norton, 1978.

heimat is an erasure of Anna Weirzbicka's explication of the concept of Heimat, taken from *Understanding Cultures through Their Key Words,* p. 158, 1997 reproduced with permission of the Licensor through PLSclear.

daughterland contains Arabic letters that spell out the first part of a truncated expression which in Arabic refers to determinism: free will vs. fate.

ح in the poem **ltd.** (letters.that.drag) refers to Jasim Nagmeldin Almagboul (1980-2007) whose life was taken in Khartoum, Sudan by El Bashir's government when a missile was launched into his bedroom killing him instantaneously at the age of 26.

& The Arabic lyrics which appear in the poem & are from a Sudanese song written by Ibrahim Al Rashid and made popular by Ibrahim Awad, titled Ya Zamen which translates to *time.*

tusk was written for Sulafa Sahel.

suitor was written for Ibtihal Ahmed.

acknowledgements

For my parents, the panther & dove,
who pushed so hard I found no choice but to write poetry.
In memory of Mahasin & Safa Agha, my oldest & youngest θείες,
for all the love you brought & shared.
In memory of Zeinab Aboulela,
who nicknamed me Shaw with her perfect blonde braids.
In memory of Zeinab Taha with her zar mermaids and cowry shell lessons.
To my sister-parent Fezome, who always set the bar, all of this exists because of you.
For Maj and Burbur, I love you boys for your light, laughter and mischief.
For my three blooming princesses, Kindah, Kayla & Kenzi.
To my giraffe of a baby brother Mustafa,
follow your beautiful heart and honor the life you choose.

My gratitude to my mentors and colleagues for their support over the years:
Linda Berger, Khalid & Lisa Garmon-Ali, Trudy Plunkett, Liz Blodgett, Molly Smith
Mullaly, Richard Golub, Michael Pratt, Lisa Flitner, Yvonne Dickerson, Terry Preston,
Sharon Potenza, Gubara Elhassan, Hafiza Abdelgadir, Naima Ibnoumanaf, Limia El
Sayed, Wathig Yousif, Younis El-Amin, Nada Wanni, M. El Khatim, Sadig Yahya, Khalid
Mahmoud, Sarah Helfa, Ali & Abu Bakr Al-Amin, Hayder Makki, Monica Adli, Halim
Faroug, Isabelle Stamatiadou, Romuald Founkoua and Yassir Hassan.

For friendship, guidance, inspiration, support and patience over the years:
Anath ElKaim, Vanessa Kelly, Natasha Burge, Xirene D'Oyen Cameron & Asilah-Naira,
Catherine Carberry, Dar Al Naim, Audre Lorde, Yannis Ritsos, Matthew Shenoda, Ladan
Osman, Ilya Kaminsky, Philip Metres, Tayeb Salih, Nawal El Saadawi, Leila Aboulela,
Jamal Mahjoub, Salim Haddad, Faisal Mohyuddin, Warsan Shire, Safia Elhillo, Marwa
Helal, Mahtem Shifferaw, Dalia El-Hassan, Najwan Darwish, Suja Sawafta, Sewit Sium,
Nadra Mabrouk, Omotara James, Akosua Zimba Afiriyie-Hwedie, Diriye Osman, Nihal
Mubarak, Noon Salah, Tim and Maryam, Nia McAllister, Elizabeth Gessel, Melissa Carr,
APBF, MOAD, Claudia Rankine, Hiwot Adilow, Itiola Jones, Evie Rice, Luis Melgarejo,
Alejandro Pedregosa, Juan Carlos Friebe, Jorge Díaz Martínez, Jeanne René Watson, Heinz
Scheuenstuhl, Khalid Abbasher, Jeremy Karn, Antonio Alfaro Sánchez, Deborah Levrier,
Fernando Grieta, Quodt Roodt, Larissa Nour Fuhrmann, Khalid Albaih, Lynne Sachs, Rob
Kenter, Marguerite Richards, Yahia Lababidi and Youssef Rakha.

31311: Sylvia & Lisa Kochinski, Alexa Bartee & Linda Esposito, Sam Yousif, Zaina
Kae, Shama Rangwala, Erin & Hillary Steen, Ms. Joanie Reis & Rebecca Daigle, Nicole
Stockenberger, Barbara Peabody & Andralee Cain, Ana Petrusevski, Rana Jarbou, Shadia
Rizvi, Sally Baalbaki, Jeni Anderson, Nida Shekhani and Saira Khan.

340341: Dina Alhusseini, Edward Washington, Danya Chebib, Nada Bokhowa, Sanja
Pupovac, Mazin Elfehaid, Marie-Adeline Paris, Cookie Moussallem and Maryam Al
Haddad.

54621: Μαρία Χρυσοπούλου, Τζων Μάρκ και Μαρίζα Μαρκούτη, Σέλμᾶ Ελτίνι & Σωκράτης,
Μαργαρίτα & Αλέξανδρος Ελ Αμίν and Fabio Casadei Turroni.

11111: Sulafa Sahel, Reem & Omnia Abbas Shawkat, Asmara Adanis, Hussam Sinada, Gassim A., Hussam Hassan, Hamid Khalafallah, Hoota El Sanosi, Ashraf Mansour, Koala & Agabani Clan, Isma'il Kushkush, Dimah & Dahlia Mahmoud, Hatim Eujayl, Menna Agha, Mawada Abu Agla, Sara Amin, Sabah 'Kiyook' El Basha, Amine Nawrani, Bashir ElShareif, Sanaa Abdelbasit, Tuna Ejaimi, Sanaa Makawi, Sarah Kamal, Pocahontas Ibnomar, Sosobenz Suleiman, Hayat El–Berair, Taher Khalifa, Seaqa Kamal, Hatim Mugdad, Betoul Mukhayer, Prayer Osman, Marwan Bashir, Jimmy Jamal, Tower, Khalid Sirelkhatim, Kinda & Ibtihal- Madea Ahmed, Teddy & Eddy Moonem, Saad Eltinay, Ghanim Al Tayeb, Hala Elhaj, Nany, Najah Ahmed, Nas with Notepads, Sara Bsonblast, Rupi Cricket Suleiman and Joel Mitchell.

75000/67000: Freddy Valle, Gala Knörr, Eric Voghel, Kandis Williams, Forrest Ann Podrat, Javiera Galvez, Belo, Shreya Dube, Charlotte Wendy Law, Anne-Sophie Aguilar and Jovanka Kalaba.

18010: Mario Pardo Segovia & Linda Stefani and Mateo, Vanessa Kelly & Bernadette Cabuay, Julie Pattou, German Faraonio, Enrique Novi, Ana Carolina Araujo, Olivia Ali Palacios, Tarek & Nadia El-Shohoumi, Zena Ballout, Andrea Kendall, Morgan Chi, Luke Hudson, Hector F. Santiago, Alice Guthrie, Mahaliya, Ismail and Nur, Ruth Giráldez Soler, Sofée Russelle, Joy Miele & Rosco, Fina Guio, Roberto Vega Morales, Seray Asker, Elsbeth Villa, Ryeanne Mantle, Ismahan Wayah, Suhaib Molina González, Leila Baroud, Andrew Barney, Lina Mansour, Ana & Chema & Emma Peinado, Yre Santiago, Sade Ferreyra, Rebecca Martínez, Tuna Belly Gomez, Yvonne & Roberto Chang, Cristina Lacalamita Raya, Chessa Fernandez & Tony Bruce Lee, Mariska Kesteloo, Kurt Schaller, Liz Barrass, Sarah, Natasha & Farah Khushi, Mona Laureys & Jan, Daniel Rosengren, Maria Forte Ruiz, Anne-Marie Huxley Miller, Rasha Arabi, Espe Jimenez, Leili Kashani, Anjali Kamat, Maher & Mazen Al Noukkari, Zeina Armanazi, Haley Stein, Rita Kakish, Adonis Kopsaphilis, Georges Daaboul, Melchor Reyes, Lotfi AlHajjam, Amina Alaoui, Mounia Atlassi, Samira Kahoul, Manal Fannane & Iru, Nour & Nella, Pablo Irurita, Sue & Miles McCarthy, Jo & Steve Baker, Ross Homaidan, Sharon Waldron, Hajji Alan, Matt & Ana Poe, Gabi Sanchez, Susana Ros, Natalie Solgala-Kaz, Marta Martínez, Sabrina Mariscal Alonso, Bryan Brown, Linda Jakubowska, Jésus García Alfaro, María Del Mar Alarcón, Patri Fernandez, Liz Shennan & Arrono, Beth Slawson, Nasser AlBreeky, Ivan Ramos & Georgia Ricchetti, Syrmo Kyrtsopoulou, Conchi & Silvia Gómez, Leyre González, Julia Sanz y Luna, Elvira Correa Al Cantara, Cristina Ramirez, Borja Capellan, José Guerrero, Carlos Martínez Aibar, Rob Stewart & Nikki Jackson, Sara Ghalia Caró, Lulla Simone, Tim Adami, Lorena Fernandez, Ana Luque, Eva & Ale Molina Saavedra, Joaquin Susino & Emilia Súnico, Yraiza Rojas, Charles Wheeler, Danielle McClellan, Kris Lindsey and Tino Ruiz & Agueda Molina & Family. I want to extend a special thank you to Valeriano Gámez and Margalit Chu, owners of Café 4 Gatos & Staff and La Fontana Restaurant & Staff for the permanent cosy spot to write.

Last but not least to the many more I carry everywhere in my heart.